Spinosaurus

by Daniel Cohen

Consultant:
Larry Dean Martin, Ph.D.
Professor-Senior Curator
Natural History Museum and Biodiversity Research Center
University of Kansas, Lawrence, Kansas

Bridgestone Books
an imprint of Capstone Press
Mankato, Minnesota

Bridgestone Books are published by Capstone Press
151 Good Counsel Drive, P.O. Box 669, Mankato, Minnesota 56002
www.capstonepress.com

Library of Congress Cataloging-in-Publication Data
Cohen, Daniel, 1936–
    Spinosaurus / by Daniel Cohen.
    p. cm.— (Discovering dinosaurs)
    Summary: Briefly describes how this dinosaur looked, what it ate, where it lived, and how
scientists learned about it.
    Includes bibliographical references and index.
    ISBN 0-7368-2526-6 (hardcover)
    1. Spinosaurus—Juvenile literature. [1. Spinosaurus. 2. Dinosaurs.] I. Title. II. Series.
QE862.S3C564 2004
567.912—dc22   2003014029

Editorial Credits
Amanda Doering, editor; Linda Clavel, series designer; Enoch Peterson, book designer and
    illustrator; Alta Schaffer, photo researcher; Karen Risch, product planning editor

Photo Credits
Brett Booth, 1, 12
Corbis/Reuters NewMedia Inc., 18
The Natural History Museum/Orbis, 4, 10, 16
OSF, 6
Photo Researchers/Joe Tucciarone/Science Photo Library, cover, 8, 14

1 2 3 4 5 6 09 08 07 06 05 04

Table of Contents

Spinosaurus compared to a
5-foot (1.5-meter) tall human

4

Spinosaurus

Spinosaurus (SPY-noh-SORE-us) was one of the largest meat-eating **dinosaurs**. It was nearly 50 feet (15 meters) long. It stood 16 feet (5 meters) tall. Spinosaurus weighed about 6 tons (5.4 metric tons). **Scientists** named spinosaurus after the tall spines sticking out of its back.

spine
a hard, sharp, pointed growth

The World of Spinosaurus

Spinosaurus lived 65 million years ago in what is now northern Africa. The climate was warmer and wetter than it is now. Today, northern Africa is very dry.

climate
the usual weather in a place

Tyrannosaurus rex

Relatives of Spinosaurus

Spinosaurus was related to other large meat-eating dinosaurs. One relative was *Tyrannosaurus rex* (ty-RAN-oh-SORE-us REX). It lived in what is now North America. *Tyrannosaurus rex* lived at the same time as spinosaurus.

What Spinosaurus Ate

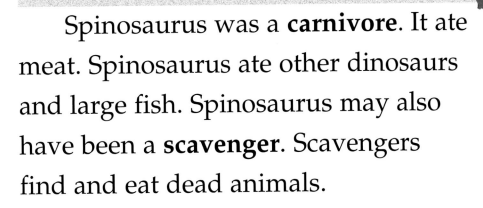

Spinosaurus was a **carnivore**. It ate meat. Spinosaurus ate other dinosaurs and large fish. Spinosaurus may also have been a **scavenger**. Scavengers find and eat dead animals.

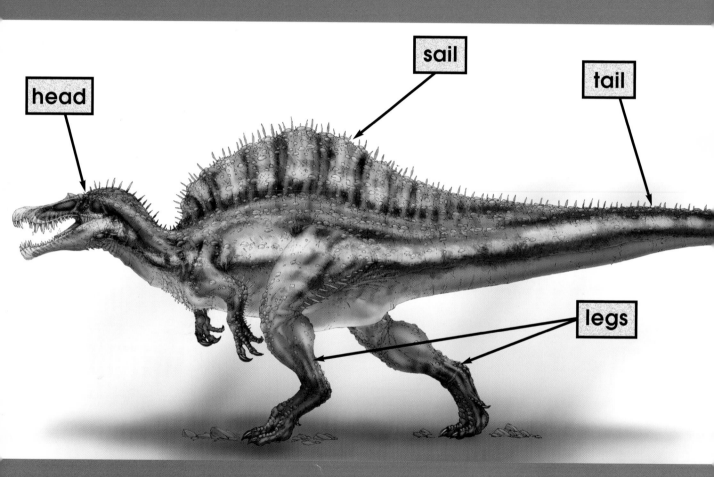

sail

tail

head

legs

Parts of Spinosaurus

Spinosaurus was a powerful dinosaur. It walked and ran on its strong back legs. It used its long, thick tail for **balance**. Spinosaurus had a large head. Sharp teeth filled its large jaws. Spinosaurus' most unusual body part was the 6-foot (1.8-meter) sail on its back.

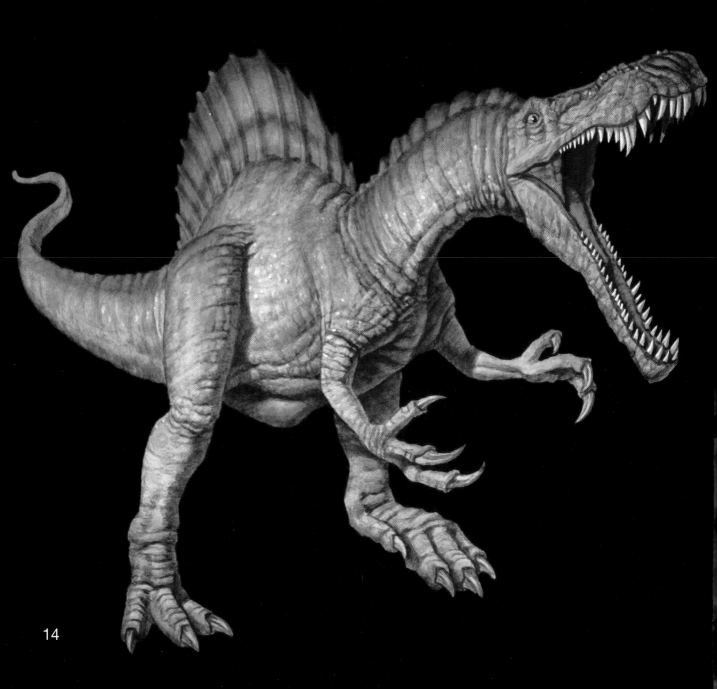

Spinosaurus' Sail

Spinosaurus' sail was made of spines. These spines grew out of its backbone. Scientists think a tough layer of skin covered the spines. The spines and skin formed a sail.

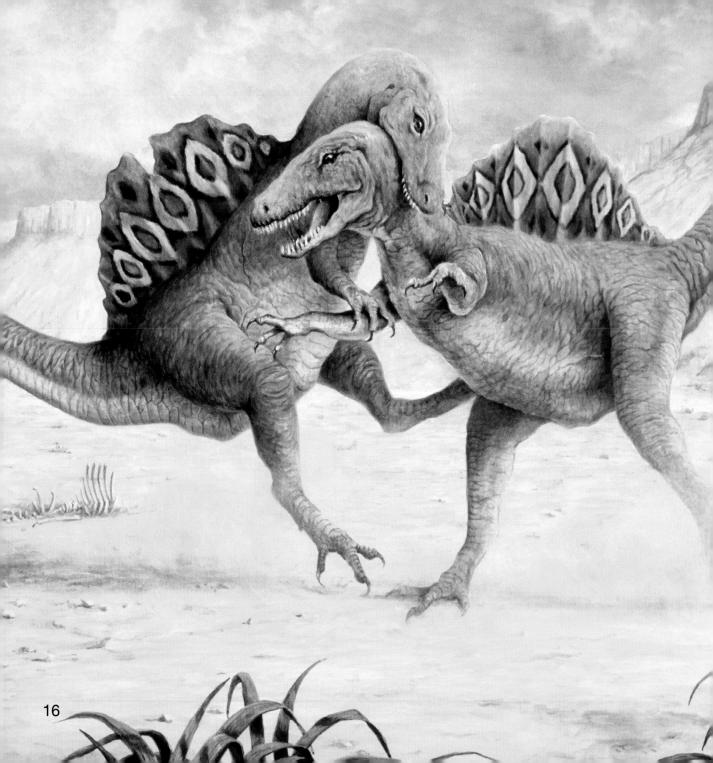

What Was the Sail For?

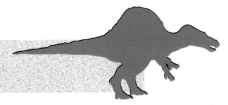

No one knows why spinosaurus had a sail. Many scientists think the sail controlled its body temperature. The sail could collect heat from sunlight. The sail may also have been used to scare away another spinosaurus during mating.

mating

when male and female animals come together to produce young

The End of Spinosaurus

Spinosaurus lived until about 65 million years ago. At that time, all the dinosaurs died out. No one knows exactly why they became **extinct**. Many scientists think that a meteorite from space hit Earth. Effects from the meteorite may have killed the dinosaurs.

meteorite
a rock from space
that falls to Earth

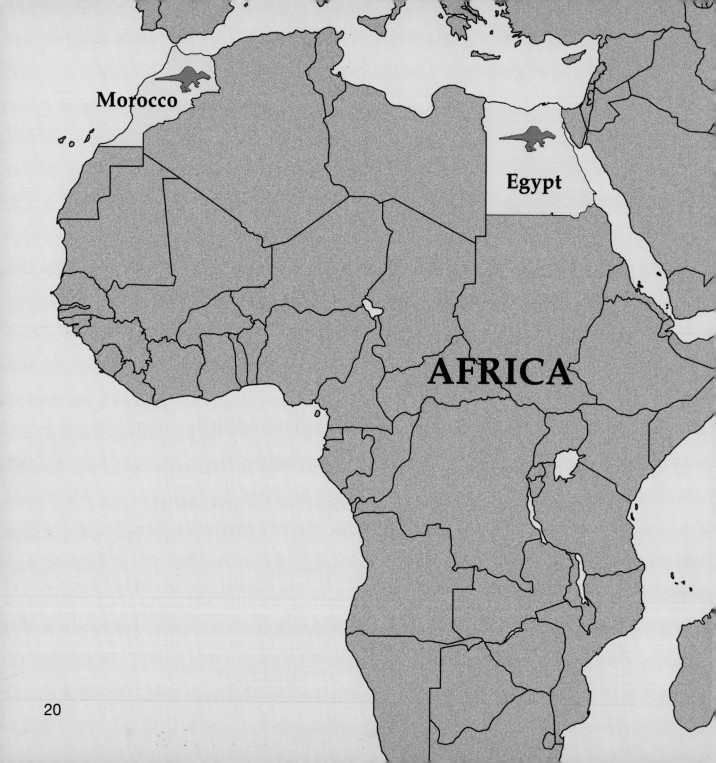

Morocco

Egypt

AFRICA

Discovering Spinosaurus

Paleontologist Ernst Stromer found the first spinosaurus **fossils** in the early 1900s. Fossils have been found in Egypt and Morocco. The most complete skeleton of spinosaurus was destroyed during World War II (1939–1945). The museum that held the skeleton was bombed.

paleontologist
a person who finds and studies fossils

Hands On: Make a Sail

Spinosaurus had a sail on its back. Try this project to make your own sail.

What You Need

2 manila file folders
scissors
paper punch
markers, crayons, or paint
glue
2 4-foot (1.2-meter) pieces of yarn or string

What You Do

1. Place one open manila folder directly over the other. Cut both folders into a spinosaurus sail shape.
2. Fold the bottom of each sail up 2 inches (5 centimeters). Above the folds, paper punch holes on both ends of each sail side.
3. Decorate the two outsides of the sail above the fold.
4. Glue the bottom of one folded side to the top of the other folded side so the sail stands up. Wait for the glue to dry.
5. Thread the yarn or string through the holes on each end of the sail.
6. Glue the tops of the sail together.
7. Tie one set of strings around your chest. Tie the other set around your waist or hips. The sail should sit on your back.

Glossary

balance (BAL-uhnss)—the ability to keep steady without falling

carnivore (KAR-nuh-vor)—an animal that eats only meat

dinosaur (DYE-na-sore)—an extinct land reptile; dinosaurs lived on Earth for more than 150 million years.

extinct (ek-STINGKT)—no longer living anywhere in the world

fossil (FOSS-uhl)—the remains or traces of something that once lived; bones and footprints can be fossils.

scavenger (SKAV-uhn-jer)—an animal that feeds on animals that are already dead

scientist (SYE-uhn-tist)—a person who studies the world around us

Read More

Barrett, Paul M. *National Geographic Dinosaurs.* Washington, D.C.: National Geographic Society, 2001.

Devillier, Christy. *Spinosaurus.* Dinosaurs. Edina, Minn.: Abdo, 2004.

Internet Sites

FactHound offers a safe, fun way to find Internet sites related to this book. All of the sites on FactHound have been researched by our staff.

Here's how:
1. Visit *www.facthound.com*
2. Type in this special code **0736825266** for age-appropriate sites. Or enter a search word related to this book for a more general search.
3. Click on the **Fetch It** button.

FactHound will fetch the best sites for you!

Index